LIGHT AND HEALTHY COOKING

Get Smart! Learn the art of healthy eating.

More and more cooks are wising up to the benefits. At cocktail parties, over meals at home and at top restaurants, it seems there is a new 'buzz' word. It describes what some good cooks are doing and the word is 'Smart'.

Smart food is high in protein, high in fibre; it is light, and energy-giving. Smart people want to eat it to be fit and to excel. Smart cooks are trimming excess fat; meat is lightly cooked and served with fresh-tasting sauces. Imaginative main dishes of vegetables are replacing meats more often in weekly menu plans. Grains are turning up in many dishes; vegetables are chosen and cooked with great care.

Today it's easy to eat the healthy way. With so many greengrocer's and supermarket shelves filled with fresh, beautiful fruits and vegetables; supermarkets, health food shops and delicatessens packed with an incredible variety of grains, seeds, oils, vinegars and exotic condiments from all over the world; butchers proudly marketing lean meat cuts, chicken shops offering a variety of poultry and fishmongers awash with fresh, shiny seafoods, there is no excuse for not serving what's right and proper to your loved ones.

Nutritionists tell us for our long-term health's sake to eat less animal fats, less salt, less sugar and to eat more fibre-rich foods. Once you start cooking from these pages you'll find it's not at all difficult, for all recipes follow these guidelines, offering a selection of dishes that will provide you with plenty of variety and enjoyment while eating them!

CONTENTS

LIGHT AND EASY FEASTS

Fresh, bright and new food ideas for light meals include fish or chicken succulently microwaved, interesting salad herbs and greens topped with a little lean protein such as grilled fresh tuna or rare beef fillet, and fabulous soups for sipping with snacks featuring low-fat dairy products.

Fish Cutlets with Spinach and Peppers

Low-fat fish quickly cooks to perfection in the microwave. For a complete meal serve with a simple rice pilau.

500g (1lb) young spinach, washed and torn into pieces

1 large red pepper, thinly sliced

4 x 155g (5oz) salmon or white fish cutlets of your choice

2 tspn fresh lemon or lime juice

Balsamic Dressing

2 tblspn balsamic vinegar

1 tblspn olive oil

1 clove garlic, crushed

freshly ground black pepper

1 To make dressing, place vinegar, oil, garlic and black pepper to taste in a screwtop jar and shake to combine. Set aside.

2 Arrange spinach and red pepper attractively on serving plates. Sprinkle with dressing and set aside.

3 Place fish in a microwavable shallow dish, sprinkle with lemon or lime juice, cover and cook on HIGH (100%) for 5-8 minutes or until flesh flakes when tested with a fork. Place fish on spinach mixture and serve immediately.

Serves 4

Creamy Curried Chicken and Leeks

Delicious served with steamed or boiled white or brown rice.

30g (1oz) butter

2 leeks, cut into thin strips

3 spring onions, sliced

4 boneless chicken breast fillets

1 tblspn plain flour

1 tspn mild curry powder

125ml (4fl oz) double cream

125ml (4fl oz) milk

1 Place butter in a microwavable casserole, cover and cook on HIGH (100%) for 45 seconds or until butter melts. Stir in leeks and spring onions.

2 Arrange chicken on top of vegetables with thicker parts towards edge of dish and cook for 5-7 minutes or until chicken is opaque. Remove chicken, set aside and keep warm.

3 Combine flour and curry powder and stir into leek mixture. Cook for 1 minute, then gradually stir in cream and milk and cook stirring once or twice, for 4-5 minutes or until mixture thickens.

4 Return chicken to dish, spoon sauce over and cook for 1-2 minutes or until chicken is cooked through.

Serves 4

Fish Cutlets with Spinach and Peppers, Creamy Curried Chicken and Leeks

Oriental Rice Salad

Serve at room temperature on its own or as a side dish with grills. Pickled ginger has a pretty pink colour and is available at health food and Oriental food stores.

750ml (1¼pt) water

315g (10oz) rice, washed

1 tblspn plus 1 tspn mirin or sweet sherry

2 eggs

pinch salt

1 tspn vegetable oil

500g (1lb) small cooked prawns, shelled and deveined, or 220g (7oz) can crab meat, drained and flaked

8-10 button mushrooms, sliced

1 young stalk celery, sliced

pickled ginger, cut into short julienne strips for garnish, optional

Sweet Vinegar Dressing

3 tblspn rice vinegar

1 tblspn vegetable oil

2 tspn sugar

1 Bring water to the boil in a heavy-based saucepan, add rice and 1 tablespoon mirin and return to the boil, stirring once. Lower heat, cover tightly and cook gently for 20-25 minutes or until rice is tender and water absorbed. Remove from heat, uncover and allow steam to escape for 2-3 minutes. Fluff up rice with a fork and set aside.

2 To make dressing, combine vinegar, oil and sugar. Spoon over warm rice and toss.

3 Beat eggs with salt and remaining mirin or sherry. Heat oil in a small saucepan and cook eggs over moderate heat, stirring, until scrambled and cooked.

4 Place rice, eggs, prawns or crab meat, mushrooms and celery in a bowl and toss. Serve garnished with ginger (if using).

Serves 4-6

Bean Thread Salad

155g (5oz) bean thread (cellophane) noodles

1 tblspn sesame oil

1 tblspn vegetable oil

2 eggs, beaten

1 unpeeled cucumber

2 boneless chicken breast fillets, poached and cut into thin strips

3 slices ham, cut into thin strips

6 spring onions, shredded

Hot Sour Sauce

1 tblspn sesame seeds

2 tblspn soy sauce

1 tblspn red chilli oil (see Kitchen Tip, this page)

2 tspn vinegar

500ml (16fl oz) chicken stock

1 Soak noodles in boiling water for 15 minutes or until soft. Drain well, toss with sesame oil and arrange on a serving plate. Chill.

2 Heat vegetable oil in a large frying pan, add eggs and cook over moderate heat to make a thin omelette. Cool, roll up and cut into thin strips.

3 Using a vegetable peeler, shave cucumber into long, thin strips. Arrange cucumber, omelette strips, chicken, ham and spring onions on noodles.

4 To make sauce, toast then grind sesame seeds in a mortar or use a blender. Add soy sauce, chilli oil, vinegar and stock and mix well. Just prior to serving, pour sauce over salad.

Serves 6

Kitchen Tip
Red chilli oil, also known as red pepper oil, can be purchased at Oriental food stores and some delicatessens. You can make it by heating 2 tablespoons vegetable oil in a small frying pan and frying 2 fresh red chillies until they turn dark. Drain the oil and store in a small jar. Or, substitute the 1 tablespoon chilli oil with a few drops of Tabasco sauce or to taste.

Vitality Cocktail

When it's too hot to cook, this quick and healthy pick-me-up is delicious served with fresh fruit and ricotta cheese-topped crispbreads.

410g (13oz) natural yogurt

500ml (16fl oz) fresh orange juice with pulp (about 6 oranges)

2 apples, roughly chopped

2 eggs

2 tblspn low-fat milk powder

Place yogurt, orange juice, apples, eggs and milk powder in a blender or food processor and process until smooth. Pour into tall glasses and serve immediately.

Serves 4

Iced Spinach and Yogurt Soup

500ml (16fl oz) chicken stock

6 spring onions, chopped

6 tender spinach leaves, stalks removed and chopped

315g (10oz) natural yogurt

1 tblspn finely chopped fresh mint

salt

freshly ground black pepper

mint sprigs or strips of lemon rind for garnish

1 Place stock in a saucepan and bring to the boil. Add spring onions and spinach. Lower heat, cover and simmer for 5 minutes or until vegetables are soft. Let cool slightly.

2 Place mixture in a blender or food processor and purée. Transfer to a bowl, cover and chill.

3 To serve, stir yogurt and chopped mint into purée. Season to taste with salt and black pepper and garnish with mint sprigs or lemon strips.

Serves 4-6

Bean Thread Salad, Iced Spinach and Yogurt Soup, Vitality Cocktail

Grilled Chicken Salad

Veal Scallopine

For light and easy feasting, serve with a tossed salad of mixed lettuces.

750g (1¹/2lb) veal escalopes (schnitzels), pounded thinly

salt

freshly ground black pepper

plain flour for dusting

1 tblspn virgin olive oil

125ml (4fl oz) chicken stock

1 tblspn butter

1 tblspn balsamic vinegar or fresh lemon juice

2-3 tblspn finely chopped fresh parsley

1 Trim veal of any fat, sprinkle with salt and black pepper and coat with flour, shaking off excess.

2 Heat oil in a large frying pan over a medium to high heat and cook veal, in batches, for 2 minutes each side or until cooked and brown. Transfer veal to a plate and keep warm.

3 Add stock to pan and boil, stirring, until liquid reduces slightly. Lower heat, stir in butter and vinegar or lemon juice and heat through. Season to taste with salt and black pepper and pour over veal. Sprinkle with parsley and serve immediately.

Serves 6

Grilled Chicken Salad

4 boneless chicken breast fillets

freshly ground black pepper

virgin olive oil

selection of salad greens such as watercress, rocket, raddichio, butter head or mignonette

30g (1oz) toasted walnuts or pecans

Balsamic Dressing

¹/4 tspn Dijon mustard

2 tblspn sherry vinegar or wine vinegar

1 tblspn balsamic vinegar

9 tblspn virgin olive oil

salt

1 Sprinkle chicken with black pepper and brush with a little oil. Cook under a preheated medium grill for 5 minutes each side or until just cooked. Cool slightly and cut into slices.

2 To make dressing, whisk together mustard and vinegars in a bowl. Gradually add oil, whisking constantly until blended and thick. Season with salt and black pepper.

3 Tear salad greens into bite-size pieces, toss with dressing and arrange on four serving plates. Top with warm chicken slices and nuts.

Serves 4

Garlic Beef with Rocket

Fat-trimmed fillet of beef served with tangy leaves of rocket is delicious dressed with garlic, balsamic vinegar and the best quality olive oil.

500g (1lb) beef fillet in one piece

2 cloves garlic, crushed

3 tblspn olive oil

salt

freshly ground black pepper

250g (8oz) rocket leaves

extra olive oil and balsamic vinegar to serve

1 Cut fillet into very thin slices. Combine garlic and olive oil in a shallow glass or ceramic dish and season to taste with salt and black pepper. Add beef slices, turn to coat and marinate at room temperature for 30 minutes.

2 Drain beef, reserving marinade and pat dry on paper towels. Heat marinade in a large frying pan over high heat and cook beef, in batches, for 1 minute each side.

3 Arrange rocket leaves on serving plates and top with beef slices. Serve immediately with extra oil and vinegar for diners to use as seasonings.

Serves 4

Grilled Tuna Carpaccio

500g (1lb) fresh tuna, thinly sliced

olive oil

2-3 leaves fresh basil, roughly chopped

2 tspn fresh oregano leaves

2 tspn fresh rosemary leaves, chopped

2-3 tblspn fresh lemon juice

salt

freshly ground black pepper

chopped fresh parsley for garnish

1 Arrange tuna on four small heatproof serving plates and drizzle with a little oil. Sprinkle with herbs, lemon juice and salt and black pepper to taste.

2 Place plates, two at a time, under a preheated medium grill and briefly cook tuna to sear the surface (tuna should be rare). Sprinkle with parsley and serve.

Serves 4

Garlic Beef with Rocket

Prosciutto, Goat's Cheese and Pears

This is a wonderful entrée or finger food and looks great served on a bed of salad greens.

100g (3¹/₂oz) goat's cheese

1 tblspn double cream

12 thin slices prosciutto or deluxe ham

2 firm-ripe pears, peeled and cut into sixths

fresh lemon juice, optional

1 Combine cheese and cream and spread over prosciutto slices to within 2cm (³/₄in) of the edge. If preparing more than one hour before serving, dip pears into lemon juice to prevent browning.

2 Place a pear wedge on each slice of prosciutto, roll up and secure with wooden toothpicks or cocktail sticks.

Serves 4 as a first course

Avocado Citrus Salad

A delicious, light, no-oil sauce made with tofu replaces a richer mayonnaise or dressing on this nutritious main dish or entrée.

2 avocados, stoned, halved and peeled

1 grapefruit, segmented

1 orange, segmented

Tofu Sesame Sauce

155g (5oz) silken tofu

2 tblspn sesame seeds, lightly toasted and ground to a paste in a mortar, or 1 tblspn Japanese sesame paste (neri-goma), at room temperature

¹/₂-³/₄ tspn sugar

¹/₄ tspn soy sauce

1 To make sauce, place tofu in a saucepan of boiling water and heat for 2-3 minutes. Drain and place in a muslin-lined colander. Place a light weight on tofu and drain for 15 minutes.

2 Place sesame seed paste and tofu in a blender or food processor and process until smooth. Add sugar and soy sauce and mix to combine.

3 Cut avocado halves into slices not quite through to stem end and place each half on a serving plate, spreading carefully to create a fan. Garnish with grapefruit and orange segments. Serve with sauce.

Serves 4

Sesame Chicken with Mango

3 boneless chicken breast fillets, cut into strips

salt

freshly ground black pepper

30g (1oz) cornflour plus 1 tblspn extra

vegetable oil for deep frying

1 tblspn soy sauce

1 tblspn rice vinegar

¹/₂ tspn dry mustard

375ml (12fl oz) chicken stock

1 tblspn chopped fresh ginger

3 cloves garlic, chopped

8 spring onions, with some green tops, chopped

12 mangetout or ¹/₂ red or green pepper, cut into long strips

1 mango, peeled and cut into strips or 400g (13oz) can mangoes, drained

2 tspn sesame oil

1 tblspn sesame seeds, toasted

1 Season chicken with salt and black pepper to taste and dust with 30g (1oz) cornflour. Heat 125ml (4fl oz) vegetable oil in a large frying pan or wok until hot. Fry chicken, in batches, for 3-4 minutes each side or until juices run clear when pierced. Drain on paper towels.

2 Combine 1 tablespoon cornflour, soy sauce, vinegar, mustard and stock in a small bowl.

3 Drain off all but 2 tablespoons oil from wok and place over a high heat. Add ginger, garlic and spring onions and stir fry for 30 seconds. Add mangetout or red pepper strips and stir fry for 2 minutes. Add mango and stock mixture and cook, stirring, for 1 minute or until mixture thickens.

4 Add chicken to pan, heat through, then stir in sesame oil and sesame seeds.

Serves 4-6

Meatball Salad with Horseradish

The combination of raw beef and horseradish is a natural in this light first course salad.

500g (1lb) lean rump steak, cubed

2 tspn chopped fresh thyme or ¹/₄ tspn dried

2 large cloves garlic, crushed

salt

freshly ground black pepper

chopped fresh parsley

assorted salad greens

1 tblspn virgin olive oil

fresh lemon juice

Horseradish Sauce

1 tblspn horseradish relish

1 tspn wine vinegar

6 tblspn sour cream or 3 tblspn sour cream and 3 tblspn double cream

1 Place steak in a food processor and process to mince. Transfer to a bowl, add thyme, garlic, salt and black pepper to taste and mix to combine. Shape mixture into walnut-size balls and toss in parsley to coat. Cover and chill thoroughly.

2 To make sauce, fold horseradish and vinegar into sour cream and season to taste with salt and black pepper. Spoon a little sauce into centre of four serving plates and arrange meatballs to one side.

3 Arrange salad greens opposite meatballs, drizzle with oil and lemon juice to taste and serve with crusty bread, if liked.

Serves 4

Ricotta Cheese with Spinach

6 spring onions, finely chopped

250g (8oz) ricotta cheese

2 tblspn mayonnaise

salt

freshly ground black pepper

8 walnut or pecan halves, toasted and roughly chopped

1/2 red pepper, chopped

8 young spinach leaves, stalks removed and finely shredded

1 Place spring onions, ricotta cheese and mayonnaise in a bowl, mix well and season to taste with salt and black pepper. Fold in nuts and red pepper.

2 Mound cheese mixture on two serving plates, garnish with spinach and serve with rye or pumpernickel bread or savoury biscuits, if liked.

Serves 2

Green Peppercorn Steak

This is a variation of steak tartare. Mince your own beef or use only a very high-quality minced steak – it should be quite peppery.

500g (1lb) lean rump steak, cubed

2 tspn green peppercorns, crushed

1 tblspn French mustard

salt

6-8 button mushrooms, finely chopped

1/2 red pepper, finely diced

1 lettuce heart, shredded

6 spring onions, finely chopped

4 tblspn thick mayonnaise

1 Mince steak cubes in a food processor and transfer to a bowl. Add peppercorns, mustard and salt to taste and mix thoroughly.

2 Shape mixture into four small patties, place on dinner plates and garnish each with small mounds of mushrooms, red pepper, lettuce, spring onions and mayonnaise.

3 Cover plates with plastic food wrap and chill thoroughly before serving. Diners mix the raw steak with the garnishes as desired.

Serves 4

Green Peppercorn Steak

Tofu, Chicken and Vegetable Sauté

Tofu is rich in vegetable protein and calcium. Now that it is so easily available from Oriental grocery stores and supermarkets, it is a worthwhile addition to a healthy diet.

1 tblspn vegetable oil

1cm (1/2in) piece fresh ginger, finely chopped

125g (4oz) lean chicken or pork mince

4 button mushrooms or 8 oyster mushrooms, sliced

1 carrot, cut into julienne sticks

300g (91/2oz) tofu, cut into small cubes and drained

2 tspn sugar

2 tblspn soy sauce

2 tblspn sake or sherry

2 spring onions, cut into 1cm (1/2in) lengths

1 egg, lightly beaten

1 Heat oil in a large frying pan or wok over high heat, add ginger and chicken or pork and stir fry, breaking up mince, for 2 minutes.

2 Add mushrooms and carrot and stir fry for 2 minutes. Add tofu and toss gently until heated through, taking care not to mash the tofu.

3 Combine sugar, soy sauce and sake or sherry and pour into wok. Add spring onions and toss gently to combine. Drizzle egg over mixture, mix lightly and remove from heat. Serve with steamed rice.

Serves 4

Mexican Olé Salad

250g (8oz) cooked or drained canned red kidney beans

1 lettuce, leaves separated and torn into bite-size pieces

1 avocado, stoned, peeled and cubed

1/2 green pepper, diced

2 tomatoes, chopped

8 crisp taco shells

125g (4oz) grated mature Cheddar cheese

dried oregano

Spicy Marinade

60ml (2fl oz) vegetable oil

2 tblspn wine vinegar

1/2 tspn ground cumin

1/2 tspn French mustard

1/4 tspn salt

pinch paprika

Vinaigrette Dressing

3 tblspn vegetable oil

1 tblspn vinegar

1 clove garlic, crushed

pinch sugar

salt

freshly ground black pepper

1 To make marinade, combine all ingredients in a screwtop jar and shake well. Combine marinade and beans in a bowl, cover and chill thoroughly.

2 To make dressing, combine all ingredients in a salad bowl and whisk until blended. Add lettuce, avocado, green pepper and tomatoes and toss well. Add undrained beans and toss to combine.

3 Spoon salad mixture into taco shells, sprinkle with cheese and oregano to taste and serve.

Serves 4

Chilled Minted Pea Soup

Should the weather turn cold you can reheat this soup and serve warm but don't add the mint and cream or yogurt until just prior to serving.

1 tblspn butter

6-8 spring onions, chopped

1 onion, finely chopped

1.2 litres (2pt) chicken stock

250g (8oz) frozen green peas

250g (8oz) diced peeled potatoes

1/2 tspn salt

1 tblspn chopped fresh mint

125ml (4fl oz) double cream or 100g (31/2oz) natural yogurt

1 Melt butter in a large saucepan over low heat, add spring onions and onion and cook until soft. Add stock, peas, potatoes and salt and bring to the boil. Lower heat and simmer for 15 minutes or until vegetables are tender. Cool slightly.

2 Place soup mixture in a blender or food processor and process until smooth. Transfer to a large bowl, cover and chill thoroughly. Just prior to serving, stir in mint and cream or yogurt.

Serves 6

Minted Lentil Salad

Be sure to use brown lentils because they hold their shape and look attractive. Serve this salad warm or chilled.

200g (61/2oz) brown lentils

sea salt

freshly ground black pepper

1/2 tspn ground cumin

1 clove garlic, crushed

100g (31/2oz) natural yogurt

125g (4oz) fresh watercress leaves or 5-6 tblspn chopped fresh parsley

11/2 tblspn chopped fresh mint

brown bread or pitta bread to serve

lettuce and tomato salad to serve

1 Soak lentils covered in boiling water for 4 hours. Alternatively, soak lentils covered with cold water overnight.

2 Drain lentils and place in a saucepan with enough fresh cold water to cover. Bring slowly to the boil, lower heat and simmer for 20 minutes or until just tender, but not mushy. Drain and place in a salad bowl.

3 Season lentils with sea salt and black pepper to taste. Add cumin, garlic, yogurt and watercress or parsley and mix well. Sprinkle with mint and serve with bread and salad.

Serves 4-6

Chilled Minted Pea Soup, Minted Lentil Salad, Mexican Olé Salad, Tofu, Chicken and Vegetable Sauté

SMART STIR FRIES

As our food preferences are changing to lighter, healthier foods we are adapting Oriental dishes to our Western tastes and using the wok to enrich menus with more varied and interesting dishes like these sumptuous stir fries – all low-fat, low-salt and higher in fibre.

Chicken in Plum Sauce

Crispy lettuce is a perfect wrap for tasty fillings. Be sure to provide finger bowls or paper towels.

500g (1lb) boneless chicken breast fillets, finely chopped

2 tblspn soy sauce

2 tblspn rice wine or dry sherry

8 tblspn Chinese plum sauce

1 tspn sugar

1 tspn cornflour

freshly ground black pepper

3 tblspn vegetable oil

5 Chinese dried mushrooms, soaked and sliced (or use fresh mushrooms)

8 canned water chestnuts, chopped

2 tblspn water

1 large cos or iceberg lettuce, leaves separated

1 Combine chicken, 1 tablespoon each soy sauce and wine or sherry, 2 tablespoons plum sauce, sugar and cornflour with black pepper to taste. Mix well and marinate for 30 minutes.

2 Heat oil in a wok over high heat and stir fry mushrooms for 30 seconds. Add chicken mixture and water chestnuts and stir fry, separating chicken, for 1 minute. Add remaining soy sauce, rice wine and water. Cook, stirring, until chicken is tender.

3 Transfer mixture to a heated serving bowl. At the table, spoon mixture into lettuce cups, drizzle with some of the remaining plum sauce then fold lettuce over filling and eat from the hand.

Serves 4-6

Thai Pork Salad

Toasted peanuts, fresh coriander or mint sprigs and sliced fresh chillies may be offered as extra toppings.

500g (1lb) boneless lean pork, finely chopped or minced

3 tblspn water

2 tblspn fresh lemon juice

2 tblspn Thai fish sauce

1/2 tspn finely sliced fresh red chilli

2 tblspn roasted peanuts

1 red onion, finely sliced

6-8 spring onions, cut into short lengths

2 tblspn finely shredded fresh ginger

6-8 fresh mint leaves

4-6 tblspn torn fresh coriander stems and leaves

8 or more cos or iceberg lettuce cups

1 Place pork and water in a large frying pan or wok and cook over moderate heat, stirring to prevent lumps forming, until pork is tender. Transfer to a salad bowl and cool.

2 Add lemon juice, fish sauce, chilli, peanuts, onions, ginger, mint and coriander to pork and mix well.

3 At the table, spoon pork mixture into lettuce cups, fold ends over filling and eat from the hand.

Serves 4-6

From left: Stir-fried Lamb in Pancakes (page 14), Thai Pork Salad, Chicken in Plum Sauce

Stir-fried Lamb in Pancakes

Pancakes can be rolled in advance and kept well covered until fried but should be eaten soon after cooking.

375g (12oz) lean lamb fillet, very thinly sliced

2 tblspn sugar

1 tblspn soy sauce

1 tspn cornflour

3 tblspn vegetable oil

1 green pepper, cut into thin strips

1/4 tspn chopped fresh red chilli

8-10 spring onions, cut into finger lengths, then shredded

2 cloves garlic, crushed

3 slices fresh ginger

1 tblspn Chinese rice wine or sherry

freshly ground black pepper

Chinese Pancakes

125g (4oz) plain flour, sifted

125ml (4fl oz) boiling water

1/2 tspn vegetable oil

1 To make pancakes, sift flour into a bowl and make a well in the centre. Add boiling water and oil and stir to make a soft but bouncy dough, adding a little extra water if necessary.

2 Shape dough into two 2.5 x 10 cm (1 x 4in) rolls. Cut each roll into four pieces and roll each piece out on a floured surface to make a 15cm (6in) round.

3 Heat a lightly greased frying pan over moderate heat and fry pancakes, one at a time, until cooked and golden. Wrap in a clean tea-towel, place on a plate or steamer over simmering water and keep warm.

4 Combine lamb, sugar, soy sauce and cornflour, mix well and set aside. Heat 1 tablespoon oil in a wok, add green pepper and chilli and stir fry for 30 seconds. Add spring onions, stir fry for 20 seconds and transfer to a bowl.

5 Place remaining oil, garlic and ginger in wok, heat until garlic sizzles then discard garlic and ginger. Add lamb mixture and stir fry for 1 minute. Return vegetables to wok, add rice wine or sherry and stir fry for 1 minute more. Season to taste with black pepper. Transfer lamb mixture to a heated serving bowl. At the table, spoon filling onto each pancake, roll up and eat from the hand.

Serves 4-6

Tofu with Broccoli

315g (10oz) tofu

3 tblspn vegetable oil

250g (8oz) broccoli, thinly sliced lengthwise

6 spring onions, cut diagonally into 2.5cm (1in) pieces

125g (4oz) button mushrooms, quartered

2 tblspn oyster sauce or soy sauce

1 tspn sesame oil

shredded spring onions or fresh coriander leaves for garnish

steamed rice to serve

1 Drain tofu on paper towels for 10 minutes, place on fresh paper towels and cut into 24 cubes.

2 Heat oil in a frying pan or wok over high heat, add broccoli, spring onions and mushrooms and stir fry for 30 seconds.

3 Add tofu to wok and stir fry gently for 2-3 minutes or until heated through. Sprinkle with oyster or soy sauce and sesame oil and stir to combine. Garnish with spring onions or coriander and serve immediately with rice.

Serves 4

Kitchen Tip
Tofu (bean curd) is very fragile, so do not stir fry vigorously. Shake or tilt the pan from time to time to baste the tofu with oil, or else turn the pieces so they can heat through evenly.

Greens with Oyster Sauce

A plate of mixed vegetables (choose the ones you like) is a good addition to an Oriental meal or to regular grills or barbecues. Served with steamed rice, this dish makes a wonderful light luncheon.

500g (1lb) green vegetables such as spinach, mangetout, Chinese cabbage, broccoli

3 tblspn vegetable oil

6 cloves garlic, chopped

3-4 tblspn fresh coriander leaves

2 tblspn oyster sauce

1 tblspn Thai fish sauce

1 tblspn cornflour blended with 60ml (2fl oz) cold water

chopped fresh coriander leaves for garnish

1 Wash vegetables. Cut leafy greens into 5cm (2in) pieces, remove strings from mangetout and cut broccoli into thin slices.

2 Heat oil in a large frying pan or wok over high heat, add garlic and stir fry for 30 seconds. Add vegetables, coriander leaves, oyster sauce, fish sauce and cornflour mixture and stir fry for 3-5 minutes or until sauce thickens and vegetables are cooked to your liking.

3 Transfer vegetables to a heated serving dish, sprinkle with chopped coriander and serve immediately.

Serves 4

Tofu With Broccoli

Stir-fried Rice

If you have Chinese rice wine, sprinkle a little over the rice just before serving to provide fragrance and flavour.

3 tblspn vegetable oil

3 spring onions, chopped

125g (4oz) button mushrooms, sliced

3 eggs, beaten

3 rashers bacon, fried and chopped

60g (2oz) small cooked and peeled prawns, optional

315g (10oz) long-grain rice, cooked and chilled

60g (2oz) frozen green peas

1 tblspn soy sauce

1 Heat oil in a large frying pan or wok over high heat, add spring onions and mushrooms and stir fry for 30 seconds. Lower heat to low, add eggs and cook, stirring, until eggs are cooked and scrambled. Transfer mixture to a heated plate and set aside.

2 Add bacon, prawns (if using), rice, peas and soy sauce to wok and stir fry for 2 minutes. Return egg mixture to wok and cook, stirring, for 1 minute longer. Serve immediately.

Serves 4

Chicken with Asparagus

For extra flavour and variety, stir fry some sliced mushrooms or diced bamboo shoots with the asparagus.

625g (1lb 4oz) boneless chicken breast fillets, cubed

1/2 egg white

1 tspn cornflour

2 tblspn Chinese rice wine or sherry

6 tblspn vegetable or light olive oil

8 spears asparagus, cut into short lengths

1 tspn salt

1/2 tspn sugar

1 Place chicken in a bowl, add egg white, cornflour and 1 tablespoon wine or sherry and mix well.

2 Heat 4 tablespoons oil in a large frying pan or wok until hot, add chicken and stir fry until opaque. Remove to a plate and wipe wok clean with paper towels.

3 Heat remaining oil in pan and stir fry asparagus for 3 minutes. Return chicken to pan, add salt, sugar and remaining wine or sherry and heat through, stirring. Serve immediately.

Serves 6

Gingered Lamb, Broccoli and Red Pepper

Any young green vegetable may be used in place of the broccoli.

2 tblspn soy sauce

2 tblspn Chinese rice wine or sherry

1 tblspn red chilli oil (see Kitchen Tip, page 4)

4 tblspn sesame oil

1 large clove garlic, chopped

2 tblspn fine julienne strips fresh ginger

1 tblspn chopped spring onion

500g (1lb) lean lamb fillet, very thinly sliced

500g (1lb) broccoli, broken into small florets

1 tspn cornflour

2 tblspn beef stock

1/2 red pepper, cut into thin strips

3-4 spring onions, cut into thin strips

1 Whisk together soy sauce, 1 tablespoon wine or sherry, chilli oil, 1 tablespoon sesame oil, garlic, ginger and chopped spring onion in a large bowl. Stir in lamb, cover and marinate in the refrigerator for at least 2 hours.

2 Blanch broccoli in boiling water for 1 minute and drain. Blend cornflour, stock and remaining wine or sherry and set aside.

3 Heat 2 tablespoons sesame oil in a large frying pan or wok over high heat, add broccoli and red pepper and stir fry for 2 minutes or until peppers are tender-crisp. Add spring onions and stir fry for 30 seconds. Using a slotted spoon, transfer mixture to a bowl.

4 Heat remaining sesame oil in wok, add lamb mixture and stir fry for 1 minute. Stir in cornflour mixture and cook, stirring, for 30 seconds or until sauce thickens. Return vegetables to pan and heat through.

Serves 4

Shredded Beef with Peppers

500g (1lb) lean beef steak, very thinly sliced

3 tblspn soy sauce

2 tblspn Chinese rice wine or dry sherry

2 cloves garlic, finely chopped

1 tspn grated fresh ginger

2 tblspn vegetable or light olive oil

2 onions, cut into eighths lengthwise

2 red peppers, cut into thin strips

1/2 fresh red chilli, chopped

1 Place beef in a bowl, add soy sauce, wine or sherry, garlic and ginger, mix well and marinate for 30 minutes.

2 Heat oil in a large frying pan or wok over high heat, add onions, red peppers and chilli and stir fry for 2-3 minutes or until peppers begin to soften.

3 Add beef mixture to wok and stir fry for 3 minutes longer or until beef is tender. Serve immediately.

Serves 4

Gingered Lamb, Broccoli and Red Pepper, Shredded Beef with Peppers, Chicken with Asparagus, Stir-fried Rice

Prawns with Mangetout

250g (8oz) peeled uncooked prawns, deveined

2 tspn cornflour

1 egg white

3 tblspn vegetable oil

2 spring onions, white part only, finely chopped

1 slice fresh ginger, finely chopped

100g (3½oz) mangetout, trimmed

½ tspn salt

1 tblspn Chinese rice wine or sherry

1 Place prawns in a bowl, add cornflour and egg white, mix well and refrigerate for 20 minutes.

2 Heat oil in a large frying pan or wok, add prawn mixture and stir fry for 1 minute. Using a slotted spoon, remove prawns and drain on paper towels.

3 Reheat oil in pan, add spring onions, ginger, mangetout and salt and stir fry for 2 minutes. Return prawns to pan, add wine or sherry and cook, stirring, for 1 minute longer.

Serves 2

Noodles with Prawns

500g (1lb) wide Chinese egg noodles

250g (8oz) peeled uncooked prawns, deveined

1 tblspn soy sauce

1 tblspn Chinese rice wine or dry sherry

1 tblspn cornflour

2 tblspn cold water

1 tblspn oyster sauce

2 tblspn vegetable oil

2 cloves garlic, crushed

1 tspn grated fresh ginger

½ Chinese cabbage, chopped

250ml (8fl oz) chicken stock

5 spring onions, chopped for garnish

1 Soak noodles in hot water for 10 minutes. Drain. Cook noodles in a saucepan of boiling water for 3-4 minutes or until tender. Drain, rinse and drain again.

2 Place prawns in a bowl, add soy sauce and wine or sherry and marinate for 15 minutes. Combine cornflour, cold water and oyster sauce and set aside.

3 Heat oil in a large frying pan or wok, add garlic and ginger and stir fry for 2-3 seconds. Add prawns and stir fry for 2 minutes. Add cabbage and stir fry for 1 minute.

4 Add stock to pan and bring to the boil. Stir in cornflour mixture and cook, stirring, until sauce thickens. Add noodles, heat through and garnish with spring onions.

Serves 4-6

Squid with Vegetables

500g (1lb) fresh or frozen squid rings, thawed

1 tblspn cornflour

1 tblspn Chinese rice wine or sherry

2 slices fresh ginger, finely chopped

15g (½oz) Chinese dried mushrooms, or wood ears (wood fungus)

4 tblspn vegetable oil

2 spring onions, cut into 2.5cm (1in) lengths

100g (3½oz) green beans, halved

100g (3½oz) broccoli, broken into florets

2 carrots, sliced

1 tspn sugar

½ tspn salt

1 tspn sesame oil

1 Pat squid dry and place in a bowl, add cornflour, wine or sherry and half the ginger, mix well and marinate for 20 minutes. Soak mushrooms or wood ears in warm water for 20 minutes, drain and slice, discarding stems.

2 Heat 2 tablespoons oil in a large frying pan or wok until hot, add remaining ginger and spring onions and stir fry for 30 seconds.

3 Add beans, broccoli, carrots and mushrooms or wood ears to pan with sugar and salt. Cook, stirring, adding a little water if necessary, for 3-4 minutes or until vegetables are crisp-tender. Remove mixture to a plate.

4 Heat remaining oil in pan until hot, add squid and stir fry for 1 minute. Return vegetables to pan, add sesame oil and heat through.

Serves 4

Pork Slices and Greens

Green beans, asparagus, green peppers or mangetout (or a mixture) are suitable alternatives to broccoli.

4 Chinese dried mushrooms

250g (8oz) boneless lean pork, finely sliced

2 tblspn soy sauce

1 tblspn Chinese rice wine or sherry

1 tblspn cornflour

1 medium head broccoli, broken into florets

3 tblspn vegetable oil

2 spring onions, cut into 2.5cm (1in) lengths

1 slice fresh ginger cut into thin strips

½ tspn salt

1 Soak mushrooms in warm water for 30 minutes. Drain and squeeze dry, discard stems and halve or quarter caps.

2 Place pork in a bowl, add soy sauce, wine or sherry and 1 teaspoon cornflour, mix well and marinate for 20 minutes. Blanch broccoli in boiling water. Drain and set aside.

3 Heat oil in a large frying pan or wok until hot, add spring onions and ginger and stir fry for 30 seconds. Add pork and stir fry until pork changes colour. Add mushrooms and salt and stir fry for 1 minute. Add broccoli.

4 Blend remaining cornflour with a little cold water, add to pan and cook, stirring, until sauce thickens. Serve immediately.

Serves 2

Pork Slices and Greens, Prawns with Mangetout, Squid with Vegetables, Noodles with Prawns

Imaginative Vegetable Meals

For a nutritious and delicious break from the traditional meat and three vegetables, place more emphasis on the vegetables – where it belongs! The recipes here are fresh and tasty, fibre-filled main meals based on winning combinations: vegetables and grains; vegetables and cheese or eggs; and vegetables with just a little lean meat or fish.

Mushroom and Leek Lasagne

A vegetable peeler is best for slicing the courgettes in this recipe.

45g (1¹/₂oz) butter

2 medium leeks, washed and finely sliced

500g (1lb) button mushrooms, sliced

4 courgettes, cut lengthwise into paper-thin slices

2 tblspn plain flour

600ml (1pt) milk

salt

freshly ground black pepper

pinch grated nutmeg

500g (1lb) lasagne sheets, cooked al dente, drained and kept warm

60g (2oz) freshly grated Parmesan cheese

250g (8oz) ricotta cheese

125ml (4fl oz) double cream, whipped until slightly thickened

1 Melt 15g (¹/₂oz) butter in a non-stick frying pan and cook leeks over low heat, stirring, for 15 minutes or until soft. Add mushrooms and cook until mushrooms give up their juices and all liquid evaporates. Set aside.

2 Drop courgettes into a saucepan of boiling water and cook for 2 minutes. Drain, rinse under cold water and drain again.

3 Melt remaining butter in a saucepan, stir in flour and cook over moderate heat for 1 minute. Blend in milk and cook, stirring constantly, until sauce boils and thickens. Season to taste with salt, black pepper and nutmeg.

4 Arrange about one-third of the lasagne sheets in a buttered ovenproof dish. Sprinkle with one-third of the Parmesan cheese. Top with half each of the courgettes, leek mixture and ricotta cheese, spooning ricotta into small dollops. Cover with half the sauce. Repeat layers. Top with remaining lasagne. Spread cream over top and sprinkle with remaining Parmesan cheese.

5 Preheat oven to 190°C (375°F/ Gas 5). Place lasagne on a baking sheet and bake for 30-40 minutes or until bubbly and golden. Cool for 10 minutes before cutting.

Serves 8

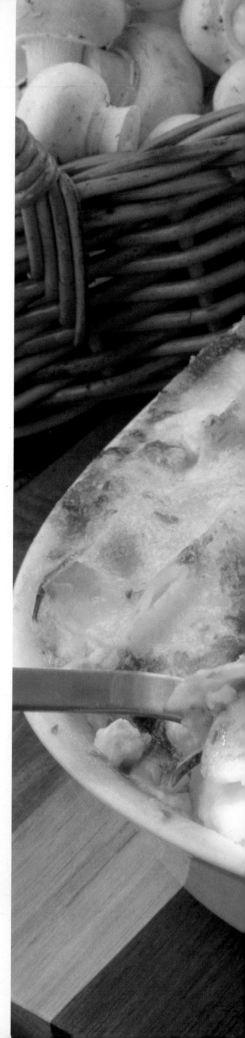

Mushroom and Leek Lasagne

Salmon Stuffed Cabbage

8 large cabbage leaves

Salmon Filling

15g (1/2oz) butter

1 onion, chopped

1 stalk celery, finely chopped

1 large potato, cooked and mashed

2 tblspn chopped fresh parsley

2 tblspn snipped fresh chives

440g (14oz) can salmon, drained

Herb and Tomato Sauce

15g (1/2oz) butter

1 onion, chopped

1 clove garlic, crushed

2 tomatoes, peeled and chopped

2 tblspn tomato purée

500ml (16fl oz) chicken stock

125ml (4fl oz) dry white wine

1/2 tspn dried marjoram

1 Blanch cabbage leaves in boiling water for 2-3 minutes or until pliable. Drain and pat dry on paper towels.

2 To make filling, melt butter in a frying pan and cook onion and celery over moderate heat for 3-4 minutes or until soft. Remove from heat, add potato, parsley, chives and salmon and mix well.

3 Preheat oven to 200°C (400°F/ Gas 6). Place a heaped spoonful of filling at the base of each cabbage leaf, fold in sides and roll up tightly to enclose filling. Arrange rolls, side by side, in a lightly buttered ovenproof dish.

4 To make sauce, melt butter in a saucepan and cook onion and garlic over moderate heat until onion is soft. Stir in tomatoes, tomato purée, stock, wine and marjoram. Bring to the boil, lower heat and simmer for 5 minutes.

5 Pour sauce over rolls and bake, basting once or twice with sauce, for 30 minutes.

Serves 4

Italian-style Stuffed Mushrooms

12 large open mushrooms

45g (11/2oz) butter

2 tblspn finely chopped spring onions

45g (11/2oz) chopped prosciutto or ham

30g (1oz) freshly grated Parmesan cheese

dried breadcrumbs and a little butter for topping

Bechamel Sauce

30g (1oz) butter

2 tblspn plain flour

250ml (8fl oz) milk

salt

freshly ground black pepper

pinch grated nutmeg

1 To make sauce, melt butter in a small saucepan, stir in flour and cook over moderate heat for 1 minute. Remove pan from heat and gradually blend in milk. Cook, stirring constantly, until sauce boils and thickens. Season to taste with salt, black pepper and nutmeg. Set aside.

2 Remove stems from mushrooms and finely chop stems. Arrange mushroom caps in a buttered shallow baking dish and set aside. Preheat oven to 250°C (500°F/Gas 9).

3 Melt butter in a small frying pan and sauté spring onions over moderate heat until golden. Add prosciutto or ham and cook, stirring, for 1 minute. Add chopped stems and salt and black pepper to taste and cook for 3 minutes longer.

4 Stir mushroom mixture and Parmesan cheese into sauce. Fill mushroom caps with mixture, sprinkle with breadcrumbs and dot with butter. Bake for 15 minutes or until topping is golden. Serve hot.

Serves 3-4

Rice and Mushroom Pie

Serve hot or cold for a family picnic or weekend meal.

4 rashers bacon, chopped

1 large onion, chopped

2 leaves fresh sage, chopped or 1/4 tspn dried

1 tspn chopped fresh thyme or 1/4 tspn dried

500g (1lb) button mushrooms, halved or quartered, if large

12 sheets filo pastry

2 tblspn vegetable oil

170g (51/2oz) rice, cooked and cooled

4 hard-boiled eggs, sliced

salt

freshly ground black pepper

1 Cook bacon and onion in a non-stick frying pan over moderate heat until onion is golden. Add herbs and mushrooms to pan and cook, stirring, for 4-5 minutes.

2 Preheat oven to 180°C (350°F/ Gas 4). Line a 23cm (9in) springform or round cake tin with 6-8 sheets of the filo, brushing every second sheet with oil.

3 Spoon one-third of the rice into prepared tin top with half the mushroom mixture then half the egg slices. Season to taste with salt and black pepper. Repeat layers and top with remaining rice. Cover filling with remaining filo, brushing every second sheet with oil. Trim edges with a sharp knife or scissors.

4 Bake pie for 35 minutes or until pastry is crisp and golden. If pastry browns too quickly, cover loosely with aluminium foil. Cool for 10 minutes before cutting.

Serves 6-8

Tomato and Cheese Soufflés

Tuna Stuffed Tomatoes

6 firm-ripe medium tomatoes

200g (6¹/₂oz) can tuna in oil, drained

125g (4oz) mayonnaise, preferably homemade with French mustard added (see recipe page 44)

fresh lemon juice

freshly ground black pepper

pinch paprika

1 tspn drained capers

assorted salad greens to serve

crusty bread to serve

1 Slice the rounded end off each tomato and, using a teaspoon, scoop out seeds and pulp, leaving a thick shell. Dice flesh finely and return to shells.

2 Combine tuna and mayonnaise and season to taste with lemon juice, black pepper and paprika. Spoon mixture into tomatoes and garnish with capers. Serve with salad greens and crusty bread.

Serves 6

Tomato and Cheese Soufflés

8 firm-ripe, small tomatoes

¹/₂ tspn salt

15g (¹/₂oz) butter

3-4 tblspn finely chopped spring onions

1 tblspn plain flour

90ml (3fl oz) milk

90g (3oz) goat's cheese, crumbled

1 egg yolk

1 tblspn chopped fresh basil

freshly ground white pepper

2 egg whites, stiffly beaten

1 Slice the rounded end off each tomato and, using a teaspoon, scoop out seeds and pulp, leaving a thick shell. Sprinkle with salt, invert on paper towels and drain for 15 minutes.

2 Preheat oven to 200°C (400°F/ Gas 6). Melt butter in a saucepan and cook spring onions over low heat until soft. Stir in flour and cook for 1 minute. Remove pan from heat and blend in milk. Cook over moderate heat, stirring constantly, until sauce boils and thickens. Cool for 5 minutes.

3 Add goat's cheese, egg yolk and basil to sauce and beat until blended. Season to taste with white pepper then fold in egg whites. Spoon mixture into shells.

4 Place tomatoes on a baking sheet and bake for 15-20 minutes or until tops are puffed and golden. Serve immediately.

Serves 8

Stuffed Baked Potatoes

If desired, use half each of the bacon and cheese for the filling and save the remainder to garnish potatoes before reheating in step 3.

4 large baking potatoes, scrubbed

60g (2oz) butter

4 rashers bacon, crisp-cooked and crumbled

60g (2oz) grated mature Cheddar cheese

freshly ground black pepper

sautéed crisp onions for garnish, optional (see Kitchen Tip, this page)

1 Preheat oven to 200°C (400°F/ Gas 6). Place potatoes, still wet, directly on oven shelf. Bake for 1 hour or until soft when pierced.

2 Cut a cross in top of potatoes, squeeze lightly and scoop pulp into a bowl. Mash pulp, add butter, bacon and cheese and mix to combine. Season to taste with black pepper.

3 Pile filling into potato shells, place on a baking sheet, sprinkle with onions (if using) and bake for 10 minutes or until heated through.

Serves 4

Kitchen Tip
Use the microwave oven to cook the onion, if liked. Cook one sliced onion in a little melted butter or oil on HIGH (100%), stirring once or twice, for 3-4 minutes.

Variations
In all variations, replace bacon and cheese with the ingredients as follows:

• **Salmon and Herb Filling:** Mix 125g (4oz) drained canned red salmon (or tuna), 3 finely chopped spring onions and 2 tablespoons chopped fresh mixed herbs into filling. Garnish with extra herbs.

• **Tomato Filling:** Mix 1 tablespoon tomato purée into filling. After reheating, sprinkle tops with breadcrumbs, drizzle with melted butter and cook under a preheated medium grill until topping is golden.

• **Spinach Filling:** Mix 4 tablespoons well drained chopped cooked spinach and a little nutmeg into filling. Sprinkle tops with grated Cheddar cheese and cook under a preheated medium grill until cheese melts.

• **Egg and Bacon Filling:** Prepare filling as recipe directs, using half the cheese. Make a hollow in top of filling, crack an egg into the hollow and sprinkle with reserved cheese. Bake in Step 3 until egg is cooked to your liking.

• **Sour Cream and Cheese Filling:** Mix 125ml (4fl oz) milk, 125g (4oz) sour cream, 1 lightly beaten egg, 4 finely chopped spring onions and 90g (3oz) grated Cheddar cheese into filling. Garnish with extra cheese.

Stuffed Baked Potatoes

Ratatouille

A microwavable vegetarian main dish.

2 courgettes, sliced

1 medium aubergine, sliced

6 tomatoes, peeled and chopped

1 green pepper, finely sliced

1 red pepper, finely sliced

1 onion, sliced

1 tblspn tomato purée

2 cloves garlic, crushed

6 tblspn olive oil

freshly ground black pepper

Combine courgettes, aubergine, tomatoes, green and red peppers, onion, tomato purée, garlic and oil in a large microwavable bowl. Cover and cook on HIGH (100%) for 15-20 minutes, stirring several times, or until vegetables are very soft. Season to taste with black pepper and cool. Serve with crusty bread.

Serves 4

Vegetable Cheese Strata

2 tblspn olive oil

2 leeks, with some green tops, washed and sliced, or 2 onions, sliced

375g (12oz) button mushrooms, sliced

2 red peppers, cut into squares

8 thick slices Italian bread, cut into cubes

125g (4oz) grated mature Cheddar cheese

60g (2oz) freshly grated Parmesan cheese

6 eggs

440ml (14fl oz) milk

1 tblspn Dijon mustard

Tabasco sauce

1 Heat oil in a frying pan over low heat and cook leeks or onions until soft. Add mushrooms and red peppers and cook, stirring, for 10-15 minutes or until peppers are tender.

2 Arrange half the bread cubes in a buttered, shallow ovenproof dish. Top with half the vegetables and sprinkle with half the cheeses. Repeat layers, spreading evenly.

3 Whisk together eggs, milk, mustard and Tabasco sauce to taste. Pour mixture evenly over strata, cover with plastic food wrap and soak for 1 hour.

4 Preheat oven to 180°C (350°F/ Gas 4). Bake strata in centre of oven for 35-40 minutes or until puffed and golden.

Serves 4

Cheese and Onion Tart

2 tblspn vegetable oil

2 onions, chopped

2 eggs

170ml (5 1/2fl oz) milk

250g (8oz) grated mature Cheddar cheese

3 rashers bacon, grilled and crumbled, optional

freshly ground black pepper

Mixed Grain Pastry

155g (5oz) wholemeal flour

125g (4oz) medium oatmeal

pinch salt

125g (4oz) butter

2-3 tblspn water

1 To make pastry, place flour, oatmeal and salt in a bowl and rub in butter until mixture resembles breadcrumbs. Mix in enough water to make a firm dough.

2 Knead dough gently on a lightly floured surface until smooth. Roll out to fit a 20cm (8in) round flan tin and chill for 15 minutes.

3 Preheat oven to 190°C (375°F/ Gas 5). Heat oil in a frying pan and cook onions over low heat until soft. Whisk together eggs and milk. Stir in onions, cheese and bacon, (if using), and season to taste with black pepper.

4 Pour filling into pastry and bake for 35-40 minutes or until pastry is golden and filling firm. Stand for 5-10 minutes before cutting.

Serves 4

Vegetable Cheddar Pie

500ml (16fl oz) milk

1 onion, finely chopped

1 bay leaf

2 sprigs fresh thyme

pinch grated nutmeg

60g (2oz) butter.

3 tblspn plain flour

125g (4oz) mature Cheddar cheese, diced

large pinch dry mustard

pinch cayenne pepper

freshly ground black pepper

750g (1lb 8oz) diced or sliced cooked mixed vegetables such as green beans, peas, carrots, corn, fennel, broccoli, cauliflower, red or green peppers, mushrooms, celery

125g (4oz) prepared puff pastry

beaten egg to glaze

1 Heat milk, onion, bay leaf, thyme and nutmeg in a saucepan over low heat until hot. Cool for 5 minutes. Remove bay leaf and thyme.

2 Melt butter in a saucepan, stir in flour and cook for 1 minute. Blend in heated milk and cook, stirring constantly, until thickened. Cool slightly. Stir in cheese and seasonings. Fold in vegetables and cool completely.

3 Preheat oven to 220°C (425°F/ Gas 7). Turn mixture into a pie dish just large enough to hold it. Roll out pastry to cover filling, trim edges and cut slits for steam. Brush with egg and bake for 10-15 minutes or until pastry is puffed and golden.

4 Lower temperature to 180°C (350°F/Gas 4) and bake for 25-30 minutes longer or until brown and bubbly. If pastry browns too quickly, cover loosely with aluminium foil.

Serves 6

Vegetable Cheese Strata

Potato Pizza

Potato Pizza

This regional Italian dish uses old potatoes mashed with olive oil and pepper as the pizza base.

1kg (2lb) old potatoes, scrubbed

125ml (4fl oz) olive oil

salt

plain flour

4 tomatoes, sliced

125g (4oz) bocconcini or fresh mozzarella cheese, sliced

75g (2¹/₂oz) freshly grated Parmesan cheese

freshly ground black pepper

black olives, halved and pitted for garnish

1 tspn fresh oregano leaves or ¹/₄ tspn dried

1 Cook potatoes in boiling salted water for 15-20 minutes or until tender. Drain and cool, peel and return to saucepan over a low heat. Add half the oil and salt to taste and mash until smooth.

2 Preheat oven to 220°C (425°F/ Gas 7). Brush a 25cm (10in) shallow baking dish with some remaining oil, sprinkle lightly with flour and spread potatoes in dish to form a base.

3 Top with tomato slices and bocconcini or mozzarella. Sprinkle with Parmesan cheese, black pepper to taste, olives and oregano. Drizzle with remaining oil. Bake for 15-20 minutes or until crust is golden and crisp.

Serves 4

Potato Spinach Gratin

500g (1lb) spinach, stalks removed and washed

60g (2oz) butter

1 large onion, finely chopped

freshly ground black pepper

1 tblspn chopped fresh dill or parsley

30g (1oz) freshly grated Parmesan cheese

500g (1lb) potatoes, peeled and sliced

2 tblspn breadcrumbs, made from stale bread

1 Place spinach in a dry saucepan, tightly cover and cook over low heat for 5 minutes or wilted. Drain, squeeze out excess moisture and finely chop.

2 Melt 30g (1oz) butter in a saucepan and cook onion for 5 minutes. Stir in spinach and black pepper to taste and cook, covered, for 5 minutes longer. Remove from heat, stir in dill or parsley and half the Parmesan cheese.

3 Preheat oven to 190°C (375°F/ Gas 5). Cook potatoes in boiling water for 5 minutes or until just tender, drain and arrange one-third of the slices in a buttered ovenproof dish. Spread spinach mixture over potatoes and top with remaining potatoes in overlapping rows.

4 Combine remaining cheese with breadcrumbs and sprinkle over potatoes. Melt remaining butter and drizzle over top. Bake for 40 minutes or until topping is golden.

Serves 4-6

Stuffed Courgettes

8 large courgettes, halved lengthwise

salt

250g (8oz) lean beef mince

1 egg

4 tblspn freshly grated Parmesan cheese plus extra for garnish

3 tblspn breadcrumbs, made from stale bread, or 45g (1½oz) rice, cooked and cooled

60g (2oz) ham, finely chopped, optional

½ tspn chopped fresh oregano or pinch dried

freshly ground black pepper

1 tblspn olive oil

1 small onion, finely chopped

4 tblspn tomato purée

2 tblspn chopped fresh basil or parsley (or a combination)

1 Scoop pulp from courgettes to make shells. Sprinkle shells with salt, invert onto paper towels and drain for 1 hour. Rinse and drain thoroughly.

2 Preheat oven to 190°C (375°F/ Gas 5). Combine beef, egg, cheese, breadcrumbs or rice, ham (if using), oregano and season with black pepper to taste. Spoon mixture into shells.

3 Heat oil in a small saucepan and cook onion for 5 minutes. Add tomato purée and basil, simmer for 5 minutes and pour into a shallow ovenproof dish.

4 Arrange shells in dish and sprinkle with extra cheese. Cover with aluminium foil and bake for 1 hour or until tender.

Serves 8

Stir-fried Summer Vegetables

2 tblspn vegetable oil

2 spring onions, sliced

1 slice fresh ginger, cut into strips

2 cloves garlic, sliced

½-1 fresh red chilli, seeded and chopped

60g (2oz) button mushrooms, sliced

125g (4oz) each baby carrots, mangetout and French beans, trimmed and cut into pieces

60g (2oz) bean sprouts

1 red pepper, sliced

2 stalks celery, sliced

2-3 broccoli or cauliflower florets

4 tblspn soy sauce

2 tblspn Chinese rice wine or sherry

1 tspn sesame oil

Heat oil in a large frying pan or wok until hot, add spring onions, ginger and garlic and stir fry for 30 seconds. Add chilli and vegetables to pan and stir fry for 2 minutes. Add soy sauce and rice wine or sherry and stir fry for 2 minutes longer or until vegetables are crisp-tender. Stir in sesame oil, mix well and serve immediately.

Serves 4-6

Stuffed Courgettes

Tuna-stuffed Pumpkin

1 medium butternut pumpkin

3 egg yolks

220g (7oz) can tuna in oil, undrained

3 tblspn freshly grated Parmesan cheese

pinch ground allspice

freshly ground black pepper

Tomato Basil Sauce

1 tblspn olive oil

1 onion, finely chopped

440g (14oz) can tomatoes, undrained and roughly chopped

1 sprig fresh basil

1 Preheat oven to 180°C (350°F/ Gas 4). Cut a thin slice from each end of pumpkin to make 'lids'. Cut pumpkin crosswise in half to form two cases. Scoop out seeds and discard, then carefully remove pulp, leaving thick shells.

2 Roughly chop pulp and place in a bowl. Mix in egg yolks, tuna with oil, 2 tablespoons cheese, allspice and black pepper to taste. Fill pumpkin shells, packing firmly.

3 Sprinkle with remaining cheese and place shells, with lids on the side, in a small ovenproof dish. Cover dish and bake for 1 hour or until shells are tender.

4 To make sauce, heat oil in a saucepan and cook onion until soft. Add tomatoes and basil and season to taste. Simmer for 15 minutes or until thick. Top shells with lids and serve with sauce.

Serves 2

Yogurt Gazpacho

410g (13oz) natural yogurt

2 cloves garlic, chopped

250ml (8fl oz) tomato juice, chilled

2 tblspn each chopped fresh parsley, mint and basil or chives

1/2 tspn ground cumin

freshly ground black pepper

125g (4oz) seeded, chopped cucumber

2 tomatoes, diced

1/2 green pepper, diced

2 stalks celery, sliced

ice cubes

sliced green olives for garnish

1 Place yogurt, garlic, tomato juice, herbs, cumin and black pepper to taste in a food processor and process to combine. Add cucumber, tomatoes, green pepper and celery and process to desired consistency. Refrigerate.

2 To serve, place several ice cubes in each serving bowl, ladle in soup and garnish with sliced olives.

Serves 6

Tuna-stuffed Pumpkin

Sweet and Sour Beans on Pumpkin Croûtes

Sweet and Sour Beans on Pumpkin Croûtes

2 x 440g (14oz) cans red kidney beans, drained

olive oil

1 onion, sliced

2 cloves garlic, crushed

1 green pepper, diced

1-2 tblspn cornflour

250ml (8fl oz) cold vegetable stock or water

1 tblspn brown sugar

2 tblspn soy sauce

1 tblspn tomato purée

1 tblspn vinegar

1 butternut pumpkin, peeled and cut into 2cm (³/₄in) thick slices

chopped fresh parsley for garnish

1 Drain beans, reserving liquid. Heat 1 tablespoon oil in a frying pan and cook onion for 5 minutes or until soft. Add garlic and green pepper and cook, stirring, for 2 minutes. Add beans and stir fry for 4 minutes.

2 Combine cornflour, stock or water, sugar, soy sauce, tomato purée and vinegar and stir into bean mixture. Simmer gently, stirring, until mixture thickens.

3 For croûtes, heat 2 tablespoons oil in a large frying pan and cook pumpkin slices over moderate heat for 4-5 minutes each side or until tender. Serve croûtes topped with beans and sprinkled with chopped parsley.

Serves 6

Broccoli Cheese Gratin

90g (3oz) unsalted butter

30g (1oz) plain flour

500ml (16fl oz) milk

125g (4oz) Gruyère or Emmenthal cheese, diced

60g (2oz) freshly grated Parmesan cheese

freshly ground white pepper

500g (1lb) broccoli, broken into florets

60g (2oz) breadcrumbs, made from stale bread

1 Preheat oven to 190°C (375°F/ Gas 5). Melt 60g (2oz) butter in a saucepan, stir in flour and cook over moderate heat for 1 minute. Blend in milk and cook, stirring, until sauce boils and thickens.

2 Remove pan from heat and stir in Gruyère or Emmenthal cheese and Parmesan cheese until melted. Season to taste with white pepper.

3 Boil, steam or microwave broccoli until just tender, drain and roughly chop. Arrange broccoli in a buttered ovenproof dish and top with cheese sauce. Sprinkle with breadcrumbs, dot with remaining butter and bake for 30 minutes or until golden.

Serves 4

LEAN AND MEATY MAIN DISHES

These dishes are ideal for gourmets who care as much about food as they do their own good health. Lean meats are grilled, roasted or pan-cooked with plenty of spicy seasonings to replace salt and served with sauces full of flavour but less rich with butter or oil.

Cutlets with Green Mustard Sauce

8 lamb cutlets, trimmed of visible fat

1 tblspn olive oil

Brown and Wild Rice

1.5 litres (2¹/₂pt) water

220g (7oz) long-grain brown rice

100g (3¹/₂oz) wild rice

1 tblspn butter, optional

freshly ground black pepper

Green Mustard Sauce

6 spring onions, with some green tops, chopped

4-6 tblspn chopped fresh coriander or parsley

250ml (8fl oz) chicken stock

1¹/₂ tblspn Dijon mustard

125g (4oz) cold butter, cubed

1 To make rice, bring water to the boil in a large saucepan, stir in brown rice, lower heat and simmer gently for 20 minutes. Add wild rice and cook for 20-25 minutes longer or until tender. Drain well, return to pan, add butter (if using) and season with black pepper. Cover and keep warm.

2 To make sauce, simmer spring onions, coriander or parsley and stock in a saucepan for 8 minutes or until liquid reduces to 2-3 tablespoons. Whisk in mustard. Add butter cubes, a few at a time, whisking constantly, over low heat until sauce is smooth. Season to taste. Strain and keep warm.

3 Brush cutlets with some oil and season with black pepper. Heat remaining oil in a large frying pan over medium to high heat and cook cutlets for 2 minutes each side or until just pink in the centre. Serve with rice and sauce.

Serves 4

Cumin Chicken

1 tblspn vegetable oil

2 tspn ground cumin

1 tspn paprika

4-6 chicken breast halves

60g (2oz) breadcrumbs, made from stale bread

3 tblspn finely chopped fresh parsley

2 tspn finely chopped garlic

freshly ground black pepper

2 tspn butter

1 Combine oil, cumin and paprika, spread over skin of chicken and marinate for 1 hour.

2 Preheat oven to 180°C (350°F/ Gas 4). Place breasts, skin side up, in a lightly oiled ovenproof dish and bake for 40 minutes. Increase temperature to 200°C (400°F/Gas 6). Combine breadcrumbs, parsley, garlic and black pepper to taste and sprinkle over chicken. Dot with butter and bake for 5 minutes or until golden.

Serves 4-6

Cutlets with Green Mustard Sauce

Roast Coriander Lamb

Serve with a favourite rice pilau and assorted sambals such as cucumber, tomato, chilli fruit pickle and sweet mango chutney.

2kg (4lb) leg of lamb
1¹/₂ tblspn fresh lemon juice
2 cloves garlic, chopped
2 tblspn vegetable oil
1 tspn ground turmeric
1 tblspn ground coriander
2 tspn ground cumin
sprigs fresh coriander for garnish

1 Using a sharp knife, score surface of lamb in a diamond pattern, cutting about 5mm (¹/₄in) deep. Combine lemon juice, garlic, oil and spices and rub mixture into lamb. Cover and refrigerate for 1 hour to allow marinade to penetrate.

2 Preheat oven to 180°C (350°F/ Gas 4). Place lamb in a roasting tin, add 250ml (8fl oz) water to tin and bake, basting occasionally with juices, for 1¹/₂ hours or until cooked to your liking.

3 Garnish lamb with coriander sprigs and serve in thick, but small slices with rice pilau and traditional curry accompaniments.

Serves 6

Meatballs with Egg Lemon Sauce

3 tblspn uncooked rice
750g (1¹/₂lb) lean beef mince
1 small onion, chopped
1 tblspn chopped fresh mint
1 tblspn chopped fresh parsley
freshly ground black pepper
375ml (12fl oz) beef stock
2 tspn cornflour
250ml (8fl oz) water
2 eggs
3-4 tblspn fresh lemon juice

1 Cook rice in a saucepan of simmering water for 10 minutes or until tender. Drain thoroughly and place in a bowl. Cool. Add beef, onion, herbs, black pepper to taste and 60ml (2fl oz) of the stock and mix well. Shape mixture into walnut-size balls.

2 Place remaining stock in a large, heavy-based frying pan and bring to the boil. Add meatballs, lower heat and simmer for 10 minutes. Blend cornflour with water, stir into stock and cook, stirring constantly, until sauce boils and thickens.

3 Beat together eggs and lemon juice until thick. Gradually stir about 250ml (8fl oz) of the hot sauce into egg mixture, then return mixture to pan, stirring constantly. Remove pan from heat, cover and stand for 5 minutes before serving.

Serves 4-6

Perfect Pan-Grilled Steak

A ribbed grill pan cooks meat on the stovetop to perfection and gives a professional looking grid pattern to the surface of the steak, however if you prefer to use the oven grill, the methods below also apply. You can purchase the meat in one piece and cut it into steaks after cooking, if wished.

4 x 185-250g (6-8oz) steaks such as boneless rump, sirloin or fillet, cut 2.5-4cm (1-1¹/₄in) thick
freshly ground black pepper
vegetable or olive oil

1 Have steaks at room temperature. Slit the fat of the rump or sirloin at intervals to prevent meat from buckling. Dry meat well on paper towels and season to taste with black pepper.

2 Place grill pan over medium to high heat, brush with oil and when pan is just beginning to smoke, add meat and cook undisturbed for 2 minutes. Rotate meat half-way around and cook for 2 minutes more to achieve a grid pattern. Turn meat over and repeat cooking and rotating as above.

3 Lower heat and continue cooking until meat is cooked to your liking. When tiny beads of pink juice appear on the surface and the meat is pliant to the touch, it is rare. When more heavily 'dewed' with juice and springy to the touch, it is medium-rare. If it is firm, it is well-done.

4 Remove steaks to heated serving plates and allow to rest for 30 seconds. Delicious served with garlic butter or a sprinkling of fresh herbs.

Serves 4

Singapore Pork Satay

This Singapore speciality can be served with a commerically prepared chilli or peanut sauce, if liked. Cook the skewers on a charcoal barbecue for the best flavour.

750g (1¹/₂lb) boneless pork loin, cut into 2.5 cm (1in) cubes
¹/₂ onion, chopped
2 cloves garlic, crushed
2 tblspn light soy sauce
1 tblspn honey
2 tspn five spice powder
freshly ground black pepper

1 Cut pork cubes in half so the chunks of meat are quite thin. Place pork in a bowl, add onion, garlic, soy sauce, honey, five spice powder and black pepper to taste and mix well. Cover and marinate in the refrigerator for 2-3 hours.

2 Thread pork onto 8 skewers and cook on a preheated medium barbecue or under a grill, turning occasionally, for 8-10 minutes or until pork is cooked through and tender.

Serves 4

Roast Coriander Lamb

Grilled Herbed Chicken

Grilled Herbed Chicken

If a grill pan is unavailable, cook fillets on a barbecue or 10cm (4in) below a preheated medium grill, turning and basting frequently with marinade.

4-6 boneless chicken breast fillets

90ml (3fl oz) olive oil

3 tblspn chopped mixed fresh herbs such as parsley, thyme, rosemary, marjoram

1 tspn finely grated lemon rind

1/2 tspn ground cumin

freshly ground black pepper

lemon wedges to serve

1 Place fillets between sheets of plastic food wrap and pound gently to flatten slightly. Combine oil, herbs, lemon rind and cumin, rub mixture over fillets and stack them in a shallow dish. Cover and marinate in the refrigerator for several hours or overnight.

2 Season fillets with black pepper to taste and cook on a heated and oiled, ribbed grill pan over medium to high heat for 2-3 minutes each side or until just firm. Serve with lemon wedges.

Serves 4-6

Pork Steaks with Lemon and Cress

4 x 125g (4oz) lean pork steaks, cut 2.5cm (1in) thick

3-4 tblspn fresh lemon juice

1/2 tspn ground cumin or coriander

1 clove garlic, crushed

freshly ground black pepper

1 tspn finely grated lemon rind

315ml (10fl oz) chicken or veal stock

250g (8oz) watercress, leaves only, finely chopped

1 tblspn crème fraîche or thick natural yogurt

1 Place pork in a shallow dish. Combine half the lemon juice, the cumin or coriander, garlic and black pepper to taste and pour over steaks. Turn steaks to coat and marinate for 1 hour.

2 Drain steaks and dry on paper towels. Heat a large frying pan over medium to high heat, brush with a little oil, add steaks and cook for 1 minute each side.

3 Add remaining lemon juice, lemon rind and half the stock to pan, lower heat and simmer gently, uncovered, for 15 minutes or until pork is tender. Transfer pork to serving plates and keep warm.

4 Add remaining stock to juices in pan and simmer until sauce thickens. Add watercress and cook for 1 minute. Stir in crème fraîche or yogurt, season to taste and heat without boiling. Pour sauce over pork and serve.

Serves 4

Chicken with Ginger Yogurt

Delicious served with Brown and Wild Rice (see recipe page 32).

315g (10oz) natural yogurt

2 tblspn finely grated fresh ginger

1/4 tspn ground turmeric

1/2 tspn ground cloves

1 tspn ground cardamom

2 tspn ground coriander

salt

freshly ground black pepper

4 boneless chicken breast fillets or 8 thigh fillets

90ml (3fl oz) double cream

1 tspn fresh lemon juice

1 Place yogurt in a shallow dish, add ginger, spices and salt and black pepper to taste and mix well. Add chicken, turning to coat, cover and refrigerate for 4 hours or overnight.

2 Scrape marinade from chicken and place in a small saucepan, with cream. Bring to the boil and boil, stirring occasionally, until reduced to 250ml (8fl oz). Add lemon juice, cover and keep warm.

3 Cook chicken on an oiled rack on a preheated medium barbecue or under a grill for 8-10 minutes each side or until tender. Serve with sauce.

Serves 4

Escalopes with Mushrooms

1 tblspn vegetable oil or butter

250g (8oz) thinly sliced veal or pork escalopes (schnitzels)

seasoned flour

125g (4oz) button mushrooms, sliced

125ml (4fl oz) chicken stock or water

1 tblspn dry sherry, brandy or vermouth

1 tblspn chopped fresh parsley

1 Heat oil or butter in a large, heavy-based frying pan. Dust escalopes (schnitzels) lightly with flour. Add to pan and cook over moderate heat for 3 minutes each side or until cooked and golden. Transfer to heated serving plates and keep warm.

2 Add mushrooms to pan with a little extra oil or butter, if needed, and sauté for 2 minutes. Add stock or water and sherry, brandy or vermouth and simmer, stirring, until liquid reduces. Spoon sauce over escalopes (schnitzels), sprinkle with parsley and serve immediately.

Serves 2

Escalopes with Mushrooms

Ham Steaks with Spiced Pears

Fresh pears may be used – peel and halve, poach in a sugar-water syrup, then proceed with the recipe.

4 x 125-185g (4-6oz) ham steaks

2 tspn vegetable oil or melted butter

Spiced Pears

6 canned pear halves in light syrup, drained, reserving syrup

125ml (4fl oz) white vinegar

4 whole allspice

¹/₂ stick cinnamon

1 To make pears, the day before using, place pears, 125ml (4fl oz) reserved syrup, vinegar and spices in a saucepan, cover and simmer for 20 minutes. Uncover and simmer for 5 minutes. Place in a bowl, cool, cover and refrigerate overnight.

2 Brush ham steaks with a little oil or butter and grill or pan-fry until heated. Transfer to serving plates and garnish each with a pear half, slicing the halves lengthwise, but not quite through to the stem end and gently fanning them out.

Serves 4

Venetian Liver with Polenta

If you like a thicker gravy, toss liver in a little seasoned flour before cooking.

vegetable or olive oil

2 large onions, finely sliced

2 tblspn water

1 tspn finely grated lemon rind

500g (1lb) calves' liver or lamb's fry, very finely sliced

freshly ground black pepper

Polenta

1.5 litres (2¹/₂pt) water

2 tspn salt

250g (8oz) finely ground corn meal (polenta)

freshly ground black pepper

1 To make polenta, bring water and salt to the boil in a saucepan. Slowly stir in polenta until smooth. Lower heat and simmer, stirring, for 45 minutes or until polenta comes away from sides of pan. Season to taste with black pepper. Turn into a greased baking dish and cool.

2 Heat 2 tablespoons oil in a large frying pan over medium to low heat. Add onions and water and mix well. Cover and cook for 20 minutes.

3 Cut polenta into squares or slices and brush lightly with oil. Place under a preheated medium grill and cook until golden on both sides. Keep warm.

4 Stir lemon rind into onions and push mixture to side of the pan. Increase heat, add a little oil then the liver. Sprinkle with black pepper and mix well, cover and cook for 2-3 minutes or until liver is tender but still pink in the centre. Spoon liver and onions over polenta.

Serves 4

Ham Steaks with Spiced Pears

Veal with Sherry Cream Sauce

Danish Meat Patties

Serve with accompaniments such as boiled potatoes, pickled cucumbers, beetroot, red cabbage and bread.

500g (1lb) lean pork mince

1 small onion, finely chopped

1 tblspn plain flour

125ml (4fl oz) soda water

1 egg, lightly beaten

freshly ground black pepper

vegetable oil

1 Place pork in a large bowl, add onion and mix well. Using hands, mix in flour, then gradually mix in water, a little at a time, until absorbed. Beat in egg and season to taste with black pepper. Cover and refrigerate for 1 hour.

2 Shape mixture into eight oval patties. Heat a large nonstick frying pan over moderate heat, lightly brush pan with oil and cook patties, in batches, for 4-5 minutes each side or until cooked.

Serves 4

Veal with Sherry Cream Sauce

2 tblspn vegetable oil

6 thick veal medallions or rib chops, rolled and tied

freshly ground black pepper

2 onions, finely sliced

3 tblspn dry sherry

250ml (8fl oz) double cream

4-6 tblspn finely chopped fresh parsley, optional

1 Heat oil in a heavy-based frying pan over moderate heat and cook veal for 1-2 minutes each side or until brown. Season to taste with black pepper.

2 Lower heat and cook gently, turning occasionally, for 15-20 minutes or until tender. Transfer to a platter and keep warm.

3 Add onions to pan with a little extra oil if needed and cook gently, stirring, for 10 minutes or until tender. Stir in sherry.

4 Add cream, bring to the boil and boil until sauce thickens. Season to taste and stir in parsley (if using). Serve sauce with veal.

Serves 6

BETTER THAN STORE BOUGHT

Homemade is better than purchased, because you've got control over the ingredients. These recipes are guaranteed fresh and free of additives, fake flavours, excessive fat or salt and offer the everyday basics, including sauces, breakfast cereals, wholesome baked treats – and some light and luscious desserts.

Fresh Curd Cheese

An old-fashioned recipe for making fresh, soft and creamy cottage cheese.

2 litres (3¹/₂pt) milk

2 tblspn natural yogurt

¹/₂ junket tablet

¹/₂ tspn salt

1 Heat milk in a saucepan just to room temperature, stir in yogurt and slowly bring to a little above blood heat, 49°C (110°F).

2 Crush junket tablet in a little water, stir into milk mixture and let stand until a curd separates from the whey and can be pulled from the sides of the pan.

3 Pour mixture into a sieve lined with a double thickness of muslin or cheesecloth and drain for at least 4 hours. For a firmer cheese place a weight over curds during draining. Stir in salt. Store covered in the refrigerator.

Makes 125g (4oz) cheese

Homemade Muesli

470g (15oz) quick-cooking oats

75g (2¹/₂oz) dried apricots, finely chopped

90g (3oz) sultanas

75g (2¹/₂oz) wheatgerm

1 tblspn raw sugar

fresh fruit and milk to serve

1 Preheat oven to 180°C (350°F/Gas 4). Place oats on a baking sheet and toast for 8-10 minutes or until golden. Cool.

2 Combine oats, fruit, wheatgerm and sugar, mix well and store in an airtight container at room temperature.

3 To serve, place 3-4 tablespoons muesli in each serving bowl, top with fruit and milk.

Makes about 750g (1lb 8oz)

Anzac Biscuits

100g (3¹/₂oz) rolled oats

125g (4oz) plain flour, sifted

90g (3oz) desiccated coconut

250g (8oz) sugar

125g (4oz) butter

2 tblspn boiling water

1 tblspn golden syrup

1 tspn bicarbonate of soda

1 Preheat oven to 180°C (350°F/Gas 4). Combine oats, flour, coconut and sugar in a bowl. Melt butter in a small saucepan over low heat, stir in water, golden syrup and bicarbonate of soda, pour mixture into dry ingredients and mix well.

2 Place spoonfuls of mixture 3cm (1¹/₄in) apart on greased baking sheets and bake for 10-15 minutes or until just firm. Stand for 3 minutes before transferring to wire racks to cool completely.

Makes about 30

Carrot Pecan Tea Cake (page 42), Anzac Biscuits, Homemade Muesli, Fresh Curd Cheese

Carrot Pecan Tea Cake

350ml (11fl oz) water
375g (12oz) sugar
30g (1oz) butter
3 medium carrots, grated
1/2 tspn ground nutmeg
1 tspn ground cloves
1 tspn salt
250g (8oz) plain flour, sifted
2 tspn baking powder
60g (2oz) chopped pecans
pecan halves for garnish

1 Preheat oven to 180°C (350°F/ Gas 4). Place water, sugar, butter, carrots, spices and salt in a saucepan and bring to the boil. Lower heat and simmer gently for 10 minutes. Cool.

2 Sift together flour and baking powder and stir into mixture with chopped nuts. Pour into a greased and floured 12.5 x 23cm (5 x 9in) loaf tin and stud batter with pecans halves.

3 Bake for 1½ hours or until cooked when tested. Stand in tin for 10 minutes before turning onto a wire rack to cool completely.

Makes one loaf

Apricot Bran Loaf

375ml (12fl oz) milk
125g (4oz) chopped dried apricots
30g (1oz) bran cereal (not flakes)
90g (3oz) brown sugar
185g (6oz) self-raising flour, sifted
1/2 tspn ground cinnamon
60g (2oz) chopped walnuts

1 Heat milk and apricots in a saucepan over low heat until warm – do not allow to simmer. Remove from heat, stir in cereal and sugar and soak for 30 minutes.

2 Preheat oven to 180°C (350°F/ Gas 4). Add flour, cinnamon and walnuts to apricot mixture, mix well and pour into a greased and lined 11 x 21cm (4½ x 8½in) loaf tin.

3 Bake for 45 minutes or until cake is cooked when tested. Stand in tin for 10 minutes before turning onto a wire rack. Cool completely. Wrap and store overnight before cutting.

Makes one loaf

Best Homemade Stock

500g (1lb) chicken backs or 1kg (2lb) shin of beef plus bones
1 stalk celery, cut into pieces
1 small carrot, cut into pieces
1 small unpeeled onion, halved
2-3 sprigs fresh parsley
1 bay leaf
4 black peppercorns

1 Rinse bones, chop if necessary and place in a large, heavy-based saucepan. Add celery, carrot, onion, parsley, bay leaf and peppercorns. Cover with cold water and bring slowly to the boil, removing scum as it accumulates. Lower heat, cover and simmer gently for 1½ hours.

2 Strain stock and cool quickly. Refrigerate stock until cold, remove fat from surface, divide stock into convenient quantities and refrigerate or freeze in suitable containers. Use as desired.

Makes 1.5-2 litres (2½-3½pt)

Quick Soup Suggestions
• **Pasta in Broth:** Bring 750ml (1½pt) stock to the boil. Add 2 tablespoons pastina (tiny pasta shapes for soup) or a handful of tortellini and simmer for 5 minutes or until pasta is tender. Add 1 teaspoon each chopped fresh parsley, red or green pepper and dry sherry. Serve sprinkled with freshly grated Parmesan cheese. Serves 2
• **Zuppa Alla Pavesi:** Fry a slice of French or Italian bread in butter until golden, place in a heated soup plate and keep warm. Bring 375ml (12fl oz) stock to the boil. Break an egg at room temperature over the bread, sprinkle with a little grated Parmesan cheese, then carefully pour hot stock over the egg to lightly poach it. Serve immediately. Serves 1

• **Mushroom Soup:** Purée 125g (4oz) roughly chopped mushrooms with 125ml (4fl oz) stock in a blender or food processor, place in a saucepan, add 375ml (12fl oz) more stock and bring to the boil. Lower heat and simmer for 2-3 minutes. Serve sprinkled with chopped fresh parsley or snipped chives. For a creamy soup, blend 2 teaspoons butter with 2 teaspoons plain flour, stir into soup and simmer until soup thickens. Just prior to serving, stir in 2 tablespoons double cream, if liked. Serves 2

Economy Tomato Sauce

2 tblspn olive oil
60g (2oz) diced carrot
1 large onion, finely chopped
90g (3oz) plain flour
600ml (1pt) chicken stock
6 tomatoes, chopped
1 tblspn tomato purée
1 tspn sugar
1 clove garlic, crushed
1 bay leaf
pinch dried basil leaves
salt
freshly ground black pepper

1 Heat oil in a large saucepan and cook carrot and onion over low heat, covered, for 5 minutes or until vegetables are soft.

2 Stir in flour and cook for 1 minute. Remove pan from heat and gradually blend in stock. Add tomatoes, tomato purée, sugar, garlic, bay leaf, basil and salt and pepper to taste. Bring to the boil.

3 Lower heat, cover and simmer, stirring, for 30-45 minutes or until thick. Cool. Discard bay leaf. Store in clean glass jars for up to 3 weeks in the refrigerator.

Makes about 600ml (20fl oz)

Apricot Bran Loaf

Homemade Mayonnaise

'Real' mayonnaise is one of the masterpieces in any good cook's repertoire; the basis for fine sauces and dressings to enhance every meal.

2 egg yolks

pinch salt

1/2 tspn French mustard

315ml (10fl oz) good quality olive oil (or half olive and half vegetable oil)

2-3 tspn white vinegar or fresh lemon juice

1 Have all ingredients at room temperature. Using a wooden spoon or wire whisk, beat egg yolks, salt and mustard in a bowl until thickened. Gradually add about 60ml (2fl oz) oil, drop by drop, beating constantly until combined. Add half the vinegar or lemon juice and beat for 1-2 minutes.

2 Gradually add remaining oil in a thin steady stream, beating constantly until mixture is thick and smooth. Beat in remaining vinegar or lemon juice. Adjust seasonings. Store in an airtight container in the refrigerator and use within 3-5 days.

Makes about 375ml (12fl oz)

Kitchen Tips
• If mayonnaise curdles and becomes thin, remedy by adding a fresh egg yolk. Beat yolk in a separate bowl and slowly whisk in the curdled mixture, beating until thick and thoroughly blended, using an extra 125ml (4fl oz) oil for the extra egg yolk.
• For a coating mayonnaise, add 2 tablespoons hot water, which will also help stabilise the sauce. For a lighter sauce, add a spoonful of natural yogurt, cream or milk.

Mayonnaise-based Sauces
For each sauce, start with 250g (8oz) mayonnaise and add the following:
• **Sauce Andalouse:** 1 tablespoon tomato purée and 1/2 finely diced green pepper. Serve with cold chicken, hard-boiled eggs, prawns or cooled, boiled new potatoes.
• **Sauce Antiboise:** 1 small clove garlic (crushed) and 1 tablespoon each finely chopped fresh parsley or chervil and fresh coriander. Serve with cold meats and chicken, potatoes, or in a mixed salad of cooked vegetables.
• **Tartare Sauce:** 1 teaspoon each finely chopped capers, pickled sweet gherkins, spring onions or shallots, green olives and 1 finely chopped hard-boiled egg white. Serve with fried or grilled fish and seafood.
• **Green Sauce:** 4-6 tablespoons very finely chopped fresh mixed herbs, such as watercress, sorrel, parsley, chives or tarragon. If using watercress or sorrel, blanch the leaves first in boiling water for 1 minute, refresh under cold water and squeeze dry in a cloth before chopping. Use sauce to coat poached fish, chicken and hard-boiled eggs.

Pep Drinks

For a quick breakfast-in-a-glass for one, or for a pick-me-up to keep you going through a full and busy day, simply combine the ingredients in a blender or food processor, blend and serve.

• **Grape and Honey Pep Drink:** 250ml (8fl oz) unsweetened grape juice and 1-2 teaspoons mild honey.
• **Slimmer's Eggnog:** 250ml (8fl oz) skim milk, 1 egg, 1 teaspoon mild honey, and 1 tablespoon dry sherry, optional.
• **Quick Pep Juice:** 1 egg and 250ml (8fl oz) unsweetened orange or other fruit juice.
• **Fruit-Nut Milk:** Finely grind 30g (1oz) nuts (almonds, pecans or walnuts) in a food processor or blender then add 250ml (8fl oz) fruit juice and 1 teaspoon mild honey and blend for 30 seconds only.

Rhubarb Orange Jam

Fresh fruit can be turned into luscious jam so easily in the microwave oven.

1.5kg (3lb) rhubarb, trimmed of leaves and finely sliced

2 tspn finely grated orange rind

4 tblspn fresh orange juice

1kg (2lb) sugar

1 Place rhubarb in a large microwavable bowl, add orange rind and juice and mix well. Cover and cook, stirring occasionally, on HIGH (100%) for 15-20 minutes or until fruit is very soft.

2 Add sugar and mix well. Cook, uncovered, for 20 minutes longer or until a little of the mixture sets when tested on a cold saucer. Cool slightly, ladle into hot sterilised jars and seal.

Makes about 1kg (2lb)

Herb Vinaigrette

A delicious dressing for tomatoes, summer salads and lightly cooked vegetables. It will keep up to a week in the refrigerator.

1 tspn Dijon mustard

1 tspn salt

1 tspn paprika

1/2 tspn freshly ground black pepper

2 cloves garlic, flattened with a heavy knife

250ml (8fl oz) vegetable or olive oil

2 tblspn tarragon vinegar

60ml (2fl oz) dry red wine

1 tspn finely chopped fresh basil, marjoram or oregano

4 tblspn chopped fresh parsley

Combine mustard, salt, paprika, black pepper and garlic in a bowl. Gradually add oil, whisking constantly until blended. Discard garlic. Beat in vinegar and wine, then stir in fresh herbs.

Makes about 315ml (10fl oz)

Blueberry Muffins

250g (8oz) plain flour, sifted

2 tspn baking powder

1 tspn bicarbonate of soda

1/2 tspn ground nutmeg or cinnamon

1/2 tspn salt

185g (6oz) demerara or raw sugar

1 egg, beaten

45g (1 1/2oz) butter, melted

185ml (6fl oz) buttermilk

125g (4oz) fresh or frozen blueberries

1 Preheat oven to 190°C (375°F/ Gas 5). Sift together flour, baking powder, bicarbonate of soda, spice and salt into a bowl. Stir in sugar.

2 Combine egg, butter and buttermilk, add to dry ingredients and stir until just moistened, taking care not to overmix. Fold in blueberries.

3 Fill muffin tins three-quarters full with batter and bake for 15-20 minutes or until muffins are cooked and golden. Serve warm with butter.

Makes 12-15

Honey Bran Muffins

375g (12oz) self-raising flour, sifted

1 tblspn baking powder

1/2 tspn bicarbonate of soda

90g (3oz) bran cereal (not flakes)

170g (5 1/2oz) sultanas

350g (11oz) honey

125g (4oz) butter, melted and cooled

2 large Granny Smith apples, peeled and grated

2 large eggs, lightly beaten

60ml (2fl oz) vegetable oil

1 Preheat oven to 190°C (375°F/ Gas 5). Sift together flour, baking powder and bicarbonate of soda into a large bowl, add cereal and sultanas and mix well. Make a well in centre of dry ingredients.

2 Combine honey, butter, apples, eggs and oil and stir into dry mixture until just moistened, taking care not to overmix.

3 Fill muffin tins three-quarters full with batter and bake for 25-30 minutes or until cooked and golden. Serve warm.

Makes 15-18

Blueberry Muffins

Lemon Cheesecake

2-3 tblspn fresh lemon juice

375g (12oz) low-fat cottage cheese or ricotta

155g (5 oz) natural yogurt

2 tblspn caster sugar

1-2 tspn finely grated lemon rind

1 tblspn gelatine

2 tblspn water

2 egg whites, beaten

lemon peel strips and extra yogurt for garnish

Muesli Base

2 egg whites

125g (4oz) toasted muesli

1 Preheat oven to 180°C (350°F/ Gas 4). To make the base, beat egg whites until stiff and fold in muesli. Press mixture evenly into base of a lightly oiled 18cm (7in) springform tin and bake for 10 minutes.

2 Place lemon juice in a blender or food processor, add cottage or ricotta cheese, yogurt and sugar and blend until smooth. Mix in lemon rind.

3 Soak gelatine in water until soft then stir over hot water until completely dissolved. Add gelatine to cheese mixture and mix well. Beat egg whites to soft peaks and fold into mixture. Pour filling over base and chill until firm – 4-5 hours or overnight. Garnish with lemon peel and extra yogurt before serving.

Serves 6

Mel I Mato

This is an adaptation of a lovely Spanish dessert.

280g (9oz) ricotta cheese

1 tblspn chopped mixed peel

4 tblspn honey

2 tblspn pine nuts, toasted

Combine cheese and peel and pile in the centre of four serving plates. Drizzle each with 1 tablespoon honey and sprinkle with pine nuts.

Serves 4

Fruity Yogurt Ice Blocks

1 tspn gelatine

1 tblspn water

2 tblspn passionfruit pulp

1 banana, puréed

1 tspn finely grated lemon rind

2 tspn fresh lemon juice

220g (7oz) low-fat natural yogurt

100g (3^{1}/$_{2}$oz) caster sugar

1 Soften gelatine in water, then stir over hot water until completely dissolved. Cool.

2 Place passionfruit pulp, banana purée, lemon rind, lemon juice, yogurt and sugar in a bowl and mix well. Stir in gelatine mixture.

3 Spoon mixture into ice-lolly (ice block) moulds or paper cups with wooden ice-lolly (ice block) sticks, cover with plastic food wrap or aluminium foil and freeze overnight or until solid.

Makes about 8

Pear and Ginger Whip

So easy and delicious, this pretty dessert is proof that healthy eating is the way to go.

2 x 440g (14oz) cans pears in natural juice, drained

155g (5^{1}/$_{2}$oz) ricotta cheese

1 tblspn honey

2 tspn preserved ginger in syrup, chopped

slivered almonds, toasted for garnish

Place pears in a blender or food processor and purée. Add ricotta cheese, honey and ginger and blend to the consistency of a mousse. Turn mixture into four serving dishes and refrigerate. Sprinkle with almonds before serving.

Serves 4

Lemon Cheesecake

Index

Managing Editor: Rachel Blackmore
Editor: Linda Venturoni
Production Manager: Anna Maguire
Picture Editor: Kirsten Holmes
Production Editor: Sheridan Packer
Trainee Production Editor: Danielle Thiris
Editorial and Production Assistant: Katrina O'Brien
Cover Styling: Donna Hay

Published by J.B. Fairfax Press Pty Limited
80-82 McLachlan Avenue
Rushcutters Bay, NSW 2011
A.C.N. 003 738 430

Formatted by J.B.Fairfax Press Pty Limited
Printed by Toppan Printing Co, Hong Kong
PRINTED IN HONG KONG

JBFP 398 A/UK
Includes Index
ISBN 1 86343 116 0 (set)
ISBN 1 86343 231 0

Distribution and Sales Enquiries
Australia: J.B. Fairfax Press Pty Limited
Ph: (02) 361 6366 Fax: (02) 360 6262
United Kingdom: J.B. Fairfax Press Limited
Ph (01933) 402330 Fax: (01933) 402234